I've Decided To Love Myself
A COLLECTION OF POEMS

iman mohsin

NFB Publishing
Buffalo, New York

ISBN: 978-1-953610-13-3

I've Decided to Love Myself/Mohsin-1st ed.

1. Poems. 2. Poetry. 3. Verse.
4. Mohsin. 5. Female Perspective.
6. Muslim-American Perspective.

NFB Publishing/Amelia Press
<<<>>>
119 Dorchester Road
Buffalo, New York 14213
For more information please visit
nfbpublishing.com

I dedicate this book to me, myself, and I.
(because I have never given up and have worked hard to love myself)

―――――――――――――――――

Special Thanks to,
My beloved Mother, my Queen. I thank you tremendously
for raising me into the amazing human being I am today. As
the Moon in the night sky, you have always been there with
an endless abundance of light, love, and strength. You mean
the universe to me. I pray that I continue to make you happy
and smile..
"I love you to the Moon and Back..."

I'd also like to thank my little sister, for always encouraging
me to be a better version of myself every day. You motivate
me to be a good role model to look up to — without you or
mom I would not have much of a drive — to be the best I
can be.

Introduction

Have you read *"A Raisin In The Sun"*? If not I encourage you
to do so, it is a play by Lorraine Hansberry, it follows the story of
a lower-class African American family living on the Southside of
Chicago during the 1950s. The family seeks to move into a home
in a white middle-class neighborhood. Below is a small snippet of
what is to come in the book, and it encouraged me to not give up
on my dream- hope you enjoy it as much as I do and get around to
reading the play.

*"What happens to a dream deferred? Does it dry up like a raisin
in the sun? Or fester like a sore--And then run? Does it stink like
rotten meat? Or crust and sugar over-- like a syrupy sweet? Maybe it
just sags like a heavy load. Or does it explode?"* —*Langston Hughes*

It is 11:00 am as I listen to this poem in my English class. It is
at that moment I realize that I must write this book. A load must
be taken off and there is so much for me to let out and say. I must
express my truest self, or my thoughts will swallow me up whole.
My thoughts and my imagination run wild and demand to be set
free, as a bird in a cage it is as though I am in an endless loop of in-
sanity that I must liberate. I do not want to grow up knowing that a
passion of mine died down when it could have been so much more
than I ever dreamed it could be. So it is at this moment I choose
to continue and pursue my dream. I pray that whoever is reading
this knows that I haven't given up on my dream and that anything
you put your mind to, you could achieve. It is crazy to think that
I wrote this three years ago, in hopes of publishing my work and
now here I am- here it is—enjoy.

Some of the Poems

"..you hesitate."

Jihad

"...When you were younger.."

Once broken & now I shine

"...I've decided to love me."

Warmth

"Indeed we belong to God.."

Helen Keller

"Greatness is within your.."

"Stop, you matter.."

"I paid the price by being nice.."

"...like a book, you're easy to read."

"Find the faults within yourself.."

"God's timing is never off…"

"A different part of me…. I was hidden away.."

Love is for all & all is to be loved.

Love

ləv/

noun

1.An intense feeling of deep affection.

Speak your mind.

even when your voice shakes.

Yell, shout

&

scream.

Let your voice be heard,

for future generations to reach.

Give them a little

something

to remember

you by.

Oh, how I have come such a long way.

On this journey of self-love.

Taking years in the making — Yet it is still a process.

(*Rome was not built in a day*)

Neither will I discover self-love in a day.

I am still learning to love myself.

It is an endless cycle of raw and tender emotion.

For the words, I thought I'd never say.

(*Silencing myself*)

I am blessed for today- writing now with a sense of tranquility.

(Finding myself)

All praise to the most merciful & most high.

I thank you, God, for saving my soul.

Guiding me and giving me the strength to endure all that I have
faced.

(*Alhamdulillah - All praise be to God, the Most Merciful and Most High*)

Walk away.
Stop forcing on a fake smile pretending like everything is okay
While inside you are falling apart.
It is okay to not be okay.
It'll be hard at first but learn to not stay.
It takes nothing to join a crowd, yet it takes
everything to walk away.

Jihad is one of the
most important tasks
for Muslims to
preserve their faith
&
To defend themselves
Against the unknown-
it could be anything difficult & challenging.
A *Jihad* is basically,
a struggle within thyself.

My biggest *Jihad*
is the continuous
fight to love me.
It is my internal conflict
That I struggle with each day
&
I'll assume that
it is safe to say,
that you may feel the same way.
So here is some advice...
Never pursue something or someone,
that is poisonous
&
drains you physically, mentally, & emotionally...
(take care of yourself)

Pills.

Medications.

The intoxication of Poisonous lies & manipulation.

When you were younger,

What did you so desperately need?

What struggles did you face?

Who did you wish was there?

Whatever the case may be,

the past is gone.

You only have today

& the future to come.

So be who you needed,

when you were younger.

Learn from your past struggles,

& mistakes.

We rise by lifting others.

So as you continue to flourish, & grow,

learn to break the cycle of,

the intoxication of medication, to blackout & block out the

manipulation, of poisonous lies, messing with your psyche.

It stumps one's growth, affecting their well being, health, & soul.

I broke my self
to complete others.
I became lost,
distorted & scared.
Feeling, utterly worthless.
I was afraid,
afraid to get hurt.
But in the end,
I realized that I allowed for the hurt.
My fears of feeling forgotten left all alone,
& left out became my reality.

I once inhaled, venomous air
that filled me up
&
suffocated me.
Lungs expanded yet mine felt like a
combustion, as if
they would collapse.
But once I walked away...
My life changed drastically.
The air I breathe is now as fresh as can be.
My lungs are filled
with clean air
&
what sadness
my heart once felt is now replaced with
happiness.
Once I was broken,
but now in the light, I shine.
(*breath*)

It takes time for people to adapt &

warm-up to others — but, it is a gift if it comes naturally.

Realize that as your strength &

harness it do not ever try to,

compromise your well being

for the happiness of others.

If they can not accept the—

the amazing person you are.

Then they do not deserve you.

You do not need them in your life.

Do we ever heal or do we just learn to cope with the hurt?

(*question*)

We all struggle, but that is the beauty of it, we all do it.

(*answer*)

The healed once were wounded & the wounded will eventually

heal.

(*wise words, that could help*)

"You know what is worse than being blind, having sight with no vision." —

Helen Keller

I held on tightly as

I hugged my past away...

Knowing that eventually, I'd have to let go.

I'd have to finally say goodbye,

— for my past, it has made,

me who I am today.

For that, I am grateful for all that I have gone through.

It has given me the strength to comfortably be myself.

(although it is still a process I am working on)

Helen Keller,

I have sight

& now can see,

the beauty that surrounds

& fulfills me.

Thank You.

"You are destined for greatness.
The only thing standing in your
way is your own doubts about yourself.."
Abdul Zaid
Said a dedicated,
caring, & passionate,
counselor to his beloved student.

For years I was hidden,
behind my own shadow.
Afraid to offend—
afraid of what I could do,
& of who I can become.
I chased after people,
I wanted acceptance, love,
&
for some odd reason redemption.

STOP,
Please, I am pleading with you to not take any pills,
you need your sleep today.
You can't numb the pain away-
You need to feel it to heal it.
I love you too much
&
I need you to *stay*.
I know it is hard but please ignore, those horrid
& wrenched thoughts that bombard your mind.
You belong.
You are loved.
You matter.
You long to be beloved by others,
But what about the love you can offer to yourself?
Your opinion is what truly matters most.
Fall in love with whomever you are.
Love yourself uncontrollably--
unconditionally, because I do.
Please know that-
You belong.
You are loved.
You matter.
You make the world a better place just by existing.
STOP,
Please, I am pleading with you to not take any pills,
you need your sleep today.
You can't numb the pain away-
You need to feel it to heal it.
I love you too much
&
I need you to *stay*.
-*A mother to her child*

I am in no need to change for you.

I am who I am because of all that I went through.

Who are you to try and change who I am because of your insecurities?

I am in no need to change for you.

If you can not handle the exquisite individual that I am, that's on you.

Looks like you need a change.

Especially if you feel the need to pinpoint others' flaws yet see no fault in your own.

Who are you to point the finger but not want to take a step back and look in the mirror?

I am in no need to change for you.

I love who I am and who I am continuously becoming.

If you can not respect, appreciate, support, or accept that, no need to stay.

Resulting in tiresome effects of trying to manipulate, gaslight, or change me.

You need to work on yourself, look in the mirror, point your finger at the reflection you see, and work hard at becoming a better individual for yourself and society.

I am in no need to change for you.

How dare you to ever, ever think that I should.

I love who I am and who I am continuously becoming.

Your weak efforts to try to change me because you're intimidated by me-

proves to me just how strong and amazing I have become and am becoming.

Religion in western media has become such,

a taboo topic that people are hesitant to 'be good'

— for the fear of becoming alienated

& Shunned.

It is quite sad-

Because society tells us to 'be ourselves'

yet that comes with rules

& regulations.

The world of today has become so cultural-

morals are diminishing-

&

Some find comfort in ignorance, just the discomfort in the knowl-

edge of right,

& wrong.

That is why many are so depressed, sad & lonely.

There is a disconnect with their lord-

& the guidance of right & wrong.

You say we're good but,

like a book, you're quite easy to read.

I suddenly feel the urge to scream.

It feels as though,

I am in an unforgiving dream.

Lost in a haze — just confused.

Through the dream, I'll wander to, &

escape the mindset of you. you. you.

Because it is tiring,

I so long to be done — with

any thought of you.

All because,

I paid the price by being nice.

Like selling dice,

to a pair of blind mice.

I became deprived,

of my basic human rights.

For example: The First Amendment

which is "my freedom of speech"

My lack of judgment became weak.

Like a kid on Halloween getting a

Trick not a Treat —

I lost myself &

suddenly became frail as in fragile.

My confidence dwindled &

the irrelevance of worry grew.

What a horrible thing to do.

For, I was too naive

& fell for you.

But as time went on,

I've come to learn that,

you were a coward and never good for me.

I eventually had the strength to let go

Falling in love with myself.

So I thank you.

Without the mistake of meeting you,

I would have never fallen in love

& met who I am today.

-9/8/18

I wound myself as I take a glimpse at my past-
Images zoom past me — I reach out and try to pick up the pieces
of my life yet as they-
Pass by they turn into sharded images like broken pieces of glass.

I was afraid to act *out*.
Hesitant to fend for me,
I resented it yet I was stuck &
I choked on my own words.

My world began to crumble,
too much happening at once.
My parents heated arguments grew,
people who I thought
we're family hurt me,
used me.
And, they tried and I mean tried,
to mentally, abuse me...
Oh, but how I grew.

God's timing is never off, never.
We are all creatures of God,
He has perfected us all.
We are just impatient.
Always wanting, asking, & demanding,
things to be & happen within an instant,
but that is not a real reality.
The real reality is facing the truth.
When you know yourself, you know God.
Seek the truth and in doing so you land in front of your lord.

It is the little things — they all add up like a domino or butterfly effect. Whether they may be good or bad. Strive to be better than you were yesterday, a week ago or even today at this given point in time. I read somewhere this quote & it now is dear to my heart.

"Don't let missing one prayer lead you to miss all five. Don't let forgetting one Surah lead you to eventually forgetting them all. Don't let one moment of sin deceive you into a habitual pattern of sins. Don't ever let a slip up be your downfall. When you are down, fall into sujood (prostration to god) And from there- watch how you will rise."

I know things are always tough at first, but with dedication & your mind made up, you can do anything & I mean anything you put your mind to. It's the little things. Day by day, one piece at a time. Like a domino or a butterfly effect. It'll be slow at first but It'll have a fast rippling outcome. Trust me the little things add up.

When we stray away from our lord,
we become fragile, our hearts harden-
& we become utterly sad.
This is because we lose our sight,
of light, what's right, &
our happiness is nowhere to be found.
When we let go of God's divine-
wisdom, Strength, & Guidance.

No matter what the circumstances
are or what situation you may be in,
or maybe facing, just turn to your lord.
He is never far away,
put your trust in him,
raise your hands- to pray.
Act as though that is your very last prayer.
Give it your all, while leaving the rest up to God.

I wanted to love,
I wanted someone,
anyone to love me,
accept me,
& just be a
A loyal friend to me.
I held on to any,
linger of hope,
I chased,
gifted,
baked,
&
ran towards,
people who never even,
deserved me.

Little did I know,
that it would be
one of the best
feelings in the world,
to be alone.
It's quite funny actually,
the thing that used to scare me,
is the thing I now love most.
It's what motivated me, being let alone,
& almost forgotten.
No one knows me anymore,
like the real version of me.
Only I do.

That empowers me.
No one ever did know me.
They only ever "knew" a part of me.
But I'm a new version,
one that I've never been before.
I'm continuously developing,
I'm growing.
I'm grown.
I'm glowing.
I radiate.
I glow.

I struggled to give up on the thought of needing

other people's love, & attention to obtaining myself-worth.

I had to take a step back &

I sat down at a table,

with past versions of myself.

Greeting them

with welcoming hellos.

As I greeted each version

of myself, I fell

deeper down the

rabbit hole.

Falling in love,

with who I have met, & seen.

Every past version of myself was of its

own uniqueness — utterly breath taken and

beautifully surreal —

The more of myself I witnessed,

the more of who I knew, I wanted to be.

I wanted to be all of the versions that — made me, me.

Without the past, I would not be,

this strong independent version of me.

The more I saw, the less I wanted for anyone,

to have the power to control or validate me.

"The worst of our faults is our interest in other people's faults"

-Ali Ibn Abi Talib

Make yourself a priority, & when you do that you'll be amazed at what you can finally accomplish, & do, especially when you focus on what is best for you.

I want the younger me to be proud of who

I've become today, for that I am proud

&

That is when I decided to love myself.

Self-love is far more important than any other form of love,

remember that.

A love for oneself is an art form of acceptance, gratitude, and

strength.

Your flaws turn into strengths & your worries turn into fuel.

You become unstoppable & no one can ever hurt you or even

come close to it,

because the most pain you have already gone through was by your

own thoughts, words & hand.

About the Author

Life as a child was not always sunshine, lollipops and rainbows — some days were cloudy, scary and sad. But I always stood tall smiling the pain away. The older I got I began to keep journals — writing down my heavy emotions, and feelings that I couldn't quite express or explain- but I knew if I wrote- it would be validated and seen. I fell in love with poetry, as I write I am able to connect with people and help them see clearly through their emotions — I am able to give advice nevertheless- allowing for them to be heard and not feel alone — something I so desperately longed for as a child.

www.ingramcontent.com/pod-product-compliance
Lightning Source LLC
Chambersburg PA
CBHW070049070426
42449CB00012BA/3201